SUCCESSFUL AMERICANS

Native Americans

Kristine Brennan

A GALLUP
RESOURCE
BOOK

Mason Crest Publishers
Philadelphia

Produced by OTTN Publishing in association with
Bow Publications, Inc.

MASON CREST PUBLISHERS INC.
370 Reed Road
Broomall, Pennsylvania 19008
(866) MCP-BOOK (toll free)
www.masoncrest.com

Printed in the United States of America.

First Printing

9 8 7 6 5 4 3 2 1

Library of Congress Cataloging-in-Publication Data

Brennan, Kristine, 1969-
  Native Americans / Kristine Brennan.
      p. cm. — (Successful Americans)
  Includes bibliographical references.
  ISBN 978-1-4222-0517-4 (hardcover)
  ISBN 978-1-4222-0866-3 (pbk.)
  1. Indians of North America—History—Juvenile literature. 2. Indians of North
America—Biography—Juvenile literature. I. Title.
  E77.4.B75 2008
  970.004'97—dc22
                                                          2008034607

Publisher's note:
All quotations in this book come from original sources, and contain the spelling
and grammatical inconsistencies of the original text.

◀ **CROSS-CURRENTS** ▶

When you see this logo, turn
to the Cross-Currents section
at the back of the book. The
Cross-Currents features explore
connections between people,
places, events, and ideas.

Table of Contents

An American Indian carries the U.S. flag at the opening ceremony of a powwow—a gathering of Native Americans that features traditional dancing and song.

CHAPTER ONE

A Painful Past, a Hopeful Present

Native Americans and First Nations people, as they are called in Canada, are not one people, but hundreds of different tribes and bands. Each group has its own culture, traditions, and language. According to the U.S. Census Bureau, the largest tribal groups in the United States are the Cherokee, Navajo, Chippewa (Ojibwa), Apache, Choctaw, Iroquois, Lumbee, Pueblo, and Sioux. The Bureau reports that there are 4.5 million people of Native American and Alaska Native heritage in the United States. This group makes up about 1.5 percent of the U.S. population.

FIRST INHABITANTS

Various groups of Native Americans have their own stories of how they came to inhabit the present-day United States. The Lakota Sioux, for instance, believe that humans lived beneath the earth's surface in a dreary, dark world. According to legend, the first man, Tokahe, was tricked into coming up to the harsh aboveground world by a spider spirit named Inktomi. Other creation stories tell not of a hostile world, but of a place made especially for the people.

Most scientists believe that the ancestors of today's Native Americans migrated from Asia to North America. As many as 20,000 years ago, they walked across a land bridge that existed at today's Bering Strait—the body of water between present-day Siberia and Alaska). The discovery of spear points in the western United States that are similar to those used thousands of years ago in Asia supports this theory.

EURO-AMERICAN CONTACT

The first contact between Native Americans and European people occurred in the 11th century, when Norse seafarers encountered indigenous people along the coast of present-day New-foundland, Canada. The Vikings called the Native American people *skraelings*. They may have been ancestors of the present-day Micmacs—the native people living in today's northeastern New England and coastal areas of Canada.

Hundreds of years later, in 1492, Christopher Columbus landed on one of the islands of today's Bahamas, southeast of present-day Florida. The discovery of what European people considered to be "The New World" led to further exploration and colonization of North America.

A portrait of explorer Christopher Columbus (1451–1506). When he reached the New World in 1492, an estimated 2 to 18 million Native Americans lived there. By 1900 conflict and disease had reduced the population to around 250,000 people in the United States and 100,000 in Canada.

During the early 1600s English settlers in the Virginia Colony established a friendly relationship with the local tribes living along the present-day Virginia coast and Chesapeake Bay area. By 1609, however, the first Powhatan War had begun between the Indians and settlers. Warfare between English colonists and local tribes ended with a 1646 treaty that established specific areas as Indian land.

From the 17th through the 19th centuries, conflicts continued to take place as whites settled on Native American land. At the same time, diseases took their toll on Indian populations. Europeans introduced new diseases to the native people that proved deadly. Smallpox is the best known of the infectious diseases that killed more than half of America's first inhabitants in widespread epidemics. Others included cholera and measles.

LOSS OF LAND

After the English colonies became the United States in 1776, the U.S. government promoted expansionism, encouraging the development of white settlements on Native American lands. Territory was either purchased or acquired through warfare. Treaties between the government and various tribes would establish specific tracts of less desirable land for Native Americans.

In 1830 the U.S. Congress passed the Indian Removal Act, which forced American Indian tribes to agree to cede lands east of the Mississippi River in exchange for payment and land in the West. Tribes of the eastern United States that refused were forcibly removed to lands west of the Mississippi River. In late 1838 the U.S. military forced the Cherokee, then living in Georgia, and the Creek, Chickasaw, Choctaw, and Seminole Indians to walk to the region now known as Oklahoma. Thousands died on the bitterly cold journey, which came to be known as the Trail of Tears. In 1851 the Indian Appropriations Act, passed by Congress, established Native American reservations in today's Oklahoma.

In the late 1830s the Cherokee were forced by the U.S. government to relocate to present-day Oklahoma. Thousands lost their lives due to disease, starvation, and exposure during the journey that became known as the Trail of Tears.

A rendering of the Battle of Little Big Horn created by an Oglala Sioux who was present at the conflict. The drawings of Amos Bad Heart Bull were published in A Pictographic History of the Oglala Sioux.

RESISTANCE

By 1870 white migration had pushed west of the Mississippi River. From 1876 to 1877, a series of conflicts known as the Black Hills War took place between the U.S. government and the Lakota Sioux and their allies. White prospectors and settlers poured into Indian lands (in today's South Dakota) when gold was found there, although a previous treaty had declared the lands off-limits to white settlers.

An important battle took place on June 25, 1876. Lakota Sioux leaders Crazy Horse and Sitting Bull led the Lakota, Cheyenne, and Arapaho in the Battle of the Little Bighorn, in today's Montana. The Indians defeated Lieutenant Colonel George Armstrong Custer and his men, who had attempted to attack their encampment. In subsequent warfare, the U.S. military ultimately forced the Indians to cede additional lands.

After 13 more years of clashes, the last major conflict between U.S. forces and American Indians took place. On December 15, 1890, Chief Sitting Bull was shot to death on the Standing Rock Reservation, in today's North Dakota. After his death, his followers fled to the Pine Ridge Reservation, in present-day South Dakota. On December 29 gunfire erupted between the sparsely armed Lakota and the soldiers at Wounded Knee Creek. Almost 300 Lakotas were killed in an attack that would later be known as the Wounded Knee Massacre.

ASSIMILATION

Wounded Knee marked the end of major Indian resistance. Native Americans faced forced assimilation into white culture. Families were ordered to send their sons and daughters to white-run government boarding schools. At these institutions children were not allowed to speak their native tongue or practice traditional ways.

Another government method for assimilating American Indians into society was the Dawes Severalty Act, passed in 1887. In effect until 1934, the law called for dividing Native American tribal land among tribe members into allotments totaling no more than 160 acres. It was thought that ownership of private property would bring tribal members into white society. However, the system, which ended the previous policy of treating tribes as sovereign nations, caused a breakdown of traditional tribal communities. In addition, the holdings were typically poor land—families that could not effectively farm the land soon lost legal ownership of it. Many allotments reverted back to the federal government, which often sold the properties to white settlers.

DISCRIMINATION

Native Americans living on reservations often suffered from a lack of health care and educational opportunities. Discrimination

Poverty and lack of opportunity have been common on most Indian reservations. The Oglala Sioux Pine Ridge Indian Reservation, in South Dakota, is no exception. Home to as many as 40,000 people, the reservation is one of the poorest places in the United States today.

against Native Americans contributed to high poverty rates on and off American Indian reservations. Many reservations lacked running water and electricity, and even schools.

Change came slowly in improving the way of life for the American Indian. Following World War I (1914–1918), in which many Native Americans served, attitudes changed. Efforts to improve living conditions on reservations were made through the Bureau of Indian Affairs (BIA), which had been established in 1824 to promote assimilation. That same year the Indian Citizenship Act was passed. This law granted full citizenship to all Native Americans in the United States. In 1934 the Indian Reorganization Act, also known as the Howard-Wheeler Act, reversed previous governmental policies. It returned some lands from federal control and encouraged tribal sovereignty and self-government.

◀ CROSS-CURRENTS ▶

Indian Americans have suffered from centuries of discrimination. To learn whether the public believes discrimination against Native Americans exists today, according to a Gallup public opinion poll, see page 51.

As of 2008 the federal government recognizes 562 Native American and Alaska Native tribes in the United States. The Bureau of Indian Affairs oversees health services, tribal courts, and other programs.

CHAPTER TWO

Ben Nighthorse Campbell: U.S. Senator

As a member of the U.S. House of Representatives and the U.S. Senate from Colorado, Ben Nighthorse Campbell championed legislation to help ranchers and Native Americans. But he has taken on many other roles in addition to that of politician, including athlete, artist, and Northern Cheyenne chief.

A TOUGH UPBRINGING

Ben Campbell was born on April 13, 1933, in Auburn, California, to impoverished parents. His father, Albert Campbell, was a grandson of Ruben Black Horse, a Northern Cheyenne warrior who had fought in the Battle of the Little Bighorn. His mother, Mary Vierra, was from Portugal.

Senator Ben Nighthorse Campbell of Colorado appears in the traditional dress of the Northern Cheyenne as he participates in groundbreaking ceremonies for the Smithsonian Institution's National Museum of the American Indian, on September 23, 1999.

Before European expansion to the west, Cheyenne tribes lived throughout the Great Plains region, from present-day Colorado to South Dakota. In the United States today, the Northern Cheyenne live in southeastern Montana, and the Southern Cheyenne can be found in central Oklahoma.

Ben's father battled alcoholism and worked sporadically, leaving Mary to care for the boy and his older sister, Alberta. Mary's tuberculosis added to the Campbell family's instability: Ben and Alberta were shuttled back and forth between their own home and an orphanage.

During his senior year Ben quit high school and worked agricultural jobs. During that time he discovered judo—a combat sport that relies on speed and leverage to throw an opponent. After getting into a fight with a young Japanese fruit-packing plant coworker who was skilled in judo, Campbell made friends with his opponent and dedicated himself to learning the sport.

Campbell served in the U.S. Air Force from 1951 to 1954. After being honorably discharged as an airman second class, he left the military with his GED (General Equivalency Diploma, which is the same as a high school diploma). He had plans for college and more judo training.

JUDO CHAMPION

Back home in California in 1954, the young veteran attended San Jose City College. As soon as Campbell established a good grade-point average he transferred to San Jose State College. There, he joined the school's judo team and his athletic career soared to new heights. During his senior year, he led his team to a 1957 state championship and a regional title.

After graduating with a degree in fine arts and physical education, Campbell moved to Japan. He wanted to compete in the Olympic Games scheduled to take place in Tokyo. So he enrolled in graduate school at Tokyo's Meiji University and trained with its judoists.

That experience helped Campbell win a gold medal at the 1963 Pan American games in Sao Paulo, Brazil. The following year, at the Olympic games in Japan, he captained the U.S. Olympic judo team. But the experience proved bittersweet: although he carried the U.S. flag at the closing ceremony, a knee injury eliminated him from the competition and ended his competitive career.

CHEYENNE ROOTS

Back in the United States Campbell opened judo studios and summer camps, in addition to working as a physical

Campbell (left) flips his judo opponent at the 1960 Pacific Amateur Athletic Competition. His determination to master the sport led to an appearance in the 1964 Olympic Games.

education teacher. In 1966 he married Linda Price, and they had two children.

In the early 1970s Campbell switched to a career in law enforcement. From 1972 to 1977, he worked as a deputy sheriff in Sacramento County, California. Being a sheriff gave Campbell the chance to meet and counsel people from all walks of life—including other Native Americans. His interest in his own heritage had been growing stronger since 1968, when he made his first visit to the Northern Cheyenne Reservation in Lame Deer, Montana.

In 1977 the Campbells moved to Ignacio, Colorado. There, at their Nighthorse Ranch, Ben and Linda raised cattle and trained horses. At the same time Ben designed and made native jewelry, a hobby his father taught him. Now, it was a lucrative career, too. He invented a style called "painted mesa," which won numerous awards at national shows.

Senator Campbell speaks to supporters of the Viva Campbell Coalition at a Denver, Colorado, rally held by Hispanic voters supporting his 2004 reelection.

FINDING POLITICS

In the spring of 1982 Campbell was set to fly out of Durango, Colorado, on jewelry business. Grounded by bad weather, he decided to attend a meeting of Democratic Party members taking place in Durango. He walked out of the meeting a Democratic candidate for a seat in the Colorado State Legislature, a seat he won that November.

Four years later, in 1986, Campbell entered national politics and was elected to the U.S. House of Representatives. On January 3, 1987, he was sworn in to the 100th Congress. Sporting western dress, complete with string tie and a ponytail, Campbell stood out from the other politicians. His fiery temper complemented his colorful image. However, Campbell's supporters didn't mind his feistiness: they re-elected him twice.

Smithsonian Institution director Lawrence Small and Ben Nighthorse Campbell, wearing Northern Cheyenne ceremonial dress, lead the Native Nations Procession on the National Mall. The event was part of the dedication of the Smithsonian's National Museum of the American Indian that took place on September 21, 2004.

U.S. SENATOR

In 1992 Campbell was elected to the U.S. Senate. During an interview, the newly elected senator explained why he planned to continue his jewelry-making business:

> I want to do public policy, but you must have something in your life outside politics. Otherwise, you get narrow, stilted tunnel vision, and that's what's wrong with Washington. We have too many professional politicians and none who do other things.

In 1997 Campbell became the first Native American to chair the Senate Committee on Indian Affairs. In that capacity he worked to secure tribal gaming reforms as well as substance-abuse prevention and treatment programs for American Indians. He also introduced legislation to fund the establishment of the National Museum of the American Indian at the Smithsonian Institution, which opened in Washington, D.C., in September 2004.

◀ **CROSS-CURRENTS** ▶

Another Native American who served as a U.S. senator and also as vice president was Charles Curtis, who was of Kaw descent. To learn more about him, turn to page 52.

In 1995 Campbell switched political parties, becoming a member of the Republican Party. He explained that his quarrels with the spending priorities of Democratic president Bill Clinton played a role in his decision. He also believed that the Democrats supported environmental causes that impeded the livelihood of ranchers, who were his constituents. Campbell would serve two consecutive terms as senator, from January 3, 1993, to January 3, 2005.

MATTERS OF PRINCIPLE

While serving in the U.S. House of Representatives, Campbell had introduced a bill to rename the Custer Battlefield National Monument. This national park, located near Crow Agency, Montana, was where the Sioux, Cheyenne, and Arapaho had defeated Lieutenant Colonel George Custer and the Seventh Cavalry. Like many other Native Americans, Campbell wondered why the monument commemorated only the battle's losing side. His bill would change the name of the Custer Battlefield National Monument to the Little Bighorn Battlefield National Monument and pay tribute to the Indians who had fought to preserve their way of life. Signed into law on December 10, 1991, the bill also called for building a memorial to the Sioux, Cheyenne, and Arapaho. When the memorial was dedicated in June 2003, Campbell was present. "It took awhile to get this done," he said, "but it is important that the Indian warriors be acknowledged and honored."

In 2004 Campbell did not seek reelection to the Senate, and instead retired. He continues to work as a celebrated jewelry designer and has also become a lobbyist working to obtain sovereignty rights for native Hawaiians. Campbell was a 2008 recipient of the Ellis Island Medal of Honor, awarded by the National Ethnic Coalition (NECO), to Americans who exemplify service and pride in their ancestry.

CHAPTER THREE

Wilma Mankiller: Cherokee Nation Chief

Wilma Pearl Mankiller, who is of Cherokee and Dutch-Irish descent, is a Native American activist and the first female chief of the Cherokee Nation. The Cherokee are the largest Native American tribe in the United States. Their land covers 7,000 square miles of Oklahoma.

MANKILLER FLATS

Wilma Mankiller was born November 18, 1945, in Talequah, Oklahoma. She joined the crowded home of Charley Mankiller and Clara Irene Sitton. Wilma was the sixth child in the family, which eventually included 11 kids. The family house, which had no phone, electricity, or running water, stood on Mankiller Flats—the 160 acres of land that was the allotment deeded by the federal government to her paternal grandfather, John Mankiller, in 1907.

The first woman elected chief of the Cherokee Nation, Wilma Mankiller.

Wilma learned the importance of community during her early years in Oklahoma, she told an interviewer:

> My early childhood in Mankiller Flats shaped the way I view the world. In that isolated, predominantly Cherokee community, . . . my parents, Charley and Irene Mankiller, my siblings, extended family, and neighbors depended on one another for support and survival. Everyone helped one another, sometimes trading eggs for milk or farm goods for store-bought goods.

IN CALIFORNIA

When Wilma was 11 years old, her father decided to join the federal Indian relocation program, which encouraged Indians to move out of reservations. In 1956 the Mankiller family moved to San Francisco, California.

Wilma hated San Francisco. Classmates laughed at her last name, and she was a disinterested student at her junior high school. During her teen years she found refuge in the San Francisco Indian Center, where the friends she made shared her Native American background.

Shortly after high school graduation, a whirlwind romance with an Ecuadorian college student named Hugo Olaya led to marriage. The young couple had two daughters—Felicia, in 1964, and Gina, in 1966.

◀ CROSS-CURRENTS ▶

The Mankiller family moved to California as part of a federal government relocation policy in effect during the 1950s. To learn more about how this program affected Wilma, turn to page 53.

As a young wife and mother in 1960s San Francisco, Mankiller became caught up in a world of political activism. On November 20, 1969, a group of Native Americans took over the site of a former maximum-security federal prison,

Alcatraz Island, in San Francisco Bay. The purpose of the takeover was to protest against the U.S. government's history of abuses against Native Americans and to call attention to problems faced by modern-day American Indians.

Mankiller would later say the 19-month takeover of the island helped ignite her political consciousness and made her an activist. "When Alcatraz occurred," she noted, "I became aware of what needed to be done to let the rest of the world know that Indians had rights too."

HOME AT LAST

Wilma's community activism led to the breakup of her marriage—she has explained that her 1974 divorce occurred because her husband wanted a traditional housewife. Two years

American Indian activists perform a traditional dance at Alcatraz Island in December 1969. Mankiller has said her desire to work for the rights of Native Americans was inspired by the protest group that took over the federal property and called for the political empowerment of American Indians.

later she moved with her daughters to Mankiller Flats, in Oklahoma, where they lived with her widowed mother. Mankiller found a job in Talequah, working at an entry-level position for the Cherokee Nation government.

In 1981 Wilma founded and became director of the Cherokee Community Development Department. In this role, she helped obtain grants and establish services for members of the tribe. One project helped the Cherokee community living in the impoverished area around Bell, Oklahoma. Many residents lived in rundown houses without running water. Mankiller raised federal and private funds and coordinated work that resulted in the construction of a water pipeline and new homes.

ENTERING POLITICS

In 1983 Ross Swimmer, who served as principal chief of the Cherokee Nation of Oklahoma, asked Mankiller to run for the position of deputy chief. Since Swimmer was far more conservative than she was, Mankiller was surprised by the invitation and initially declined. When she eventually agreed to be Swimmer's running mate, many Cherokees were skeptical—and not because of Mankiller's liberal politics. They were concerned because she was a woman—the idea that a woman could serve as a leader ran counter to the Cherokee tribal culture.

THE CHEROKEE

Until the early 1600s the Cherokee people lived in eastern and southeastern parts of the United States. Expanding European settlement pushed them westward. In the 1830s the U.S. government forced the Cherokee to resettle in modern-day Oklahoma. Today, the government of the Cherokee Nation is based in Tahlequah, Oklahoma.

A young Wilma Mankiller poses in front of the tribal emblem of the Cherokee Nation. After nearly dying in a serious car crash in 1979 and struggling with a diagnosis of myasthenia gravis, she reevaluated her life. By 1981 she had decided to commit to working on projects that would improve the lives of her people.

Mankiller responded to the uproar by knocking on doors and going out of her way to talk with people. Her campaigning efforts worked. She won a July 16 runoff election for deputy chief. Two years later, in 1985, Chief Swimmer stepped down to head the Bureau of Indian Affairs and the deputy chief became the principal chief of the Cherokee Nation.

PRINCIPAL CHIEF

On December 14, 1985, Mankiller was sworn in as the first female chief of the Cherokee Nation. "I didn't have a mandate, obviously," she later told the *Cherokee Observer*, adding that she spent the rest of Swimmer's term "just coping and trying to keep things together."

Outside Talequah, however, the first female Cherokee chief became a celebrity. Gloria Steinem, cofounder of the feminist publication *Ms.* magazine, named Mankiller the *Ms.* magazine Woman of the Year for 1987. Eventually Wilma's even temper and quiet determination won over skeptics in her homeland. In 1987, she was elected in her own right to the position of principal chief.

In 1990, during her first full term as chief, Mankiller was hospitalized with polycystic kidney disease, the same illness that had killed her father in the early 1970s. Mankiller inherited the disorder, which is characterized by the growth of numerous cysts in the kidneys. When her kidneys failed, she underwent lifesaving transplant surgery, with a kidney donated by her older brother Don.

Wilma had recovered sufficiently by 1991, when she clinched 83 percent of the vote in her bid for reelection. She served out that term, but in the spring of 1994 told her tearful staff that she would not run again.

Many people praised Mankiller for helping to revitalize the Cherokee Nation. During her 10 years as chief, tribal enrollment had increased from 55,000 to 156,000. The budget had grown from $44 million in 1986 to $86 million in 1994. While chief, Mankiller had also launched three new tribal health centers and nine new programs for children. She would later say she helped rebuild her nation "community by community and person by person."

ONGOING BATTLES

Mankiller became a teacher and lecturer. In 1996 she was on a fellowship at Dartmouth College, in New Hampshire, when she came down with pneumonia. In the hospital, Mankiller learned that she also had lymphoma, a type of blood cancer. She beat the disease the same year that Bill Clinton presented her with the Presidential Medal of Freedom, in 1998, in honor of her service to the Cherokee Nation.

In January 1998 President Bill Clinton presented Mankiller with a Presidential Medal of Freedom, the nation's highest civilian award in the United States, for her accomplishments as principal chief.

Wilma Mankiller continues to work in community development and higher education. Her books include an autobiography entitled *Mankiller: A Chief and Her People*, published in 1994, and *Every Day Is a Good Day: Reflections by Contemporary Indigenous Women,* published in 2004. She has been married to her second husband, Charlie Soap, since 1986.

CHAPTER FOUR

Louise Erdrich: Author

Louise Erdrich is an award-winning novelist of Ojibwa (Chippewa) and German descent. She has also written books of poetry, children's books, and a memoir. Many of Erdrich's books explore interactions between whites and Native Americans. They also deal with the painful past of Native Americans forced to give up the old ways to survive in the white world. She has said her stories occur in places "where cultures mix and collide."

EARLY YEARS

Born on June 7, 1954, in Little Falls, Minnesota, Louise grew up in the small town of Wahpeton, North Dakota. Six brothers and sisters would join the family after her birth. Her father, Ralph Louis Erdrich, was German-American. Her mother, Rita Gourneau, was French-Chippewa and a member of the Turtle Mountain Band of Chippewa.

Both parents worked in the Bureau of Indian Affairs boarding school in Wahpeton. As she was growing up, young Louise spent a lot of time visiting her mother's parents, who lived on the nearby Turtle Mountain Reservation.

SEARCH FOR IDENTITY

After graduating from high school in 1972, Louise enrolled at Dartmouth College, in Hanover, New Hampshire. There, she took classes in the newly established Native American studies department, headed by anthropologist Michael Dorris.

While at Dartmouth, Erdrich took on a various jobs that she would later say helped her experience life. She worked as a lifeguard, waitress, poetry teacher in prisons, and construction flag signaler. She also became an editor for a Boston Indian Council newspaper called *The Circle*. The newspaper job helped her understand that she wanted to write about searching for the Native American identity, she told an interviewer:

> Settling into that job and becoming comfortable with an urban community—which is very different from the reservation community—gave me another reference point. There were lots of people with mixed blood, lots of people who had their own confusions. I realized that this was part of my life—it wasn't something that I was making up—and that it was something I *wanted* to write about.

Minnesota-born Louise Erdrich, who is a member of the Turtle Mountain Band of Chippewa, is an award-winning novelist and poet.

Louise Erdrich: Author

The Ojibwa, or Chippewa (also known as the Anishinaabe Nation), were once one of the largest Great Lakes tribes. Today Ojibwa reservations exist in Michigan, Minnesota, North Dakota, Wisconsin, and Montana, as well as in parts of Canada. The Ojibwa tribe is the third-largest Native American group in the United States.

When he married Erdrich in 1981, Michael Dorris was a single father—the adoptive parent of three Native American children.

In 1976 Erdrich received her bachelor of arts degree from Dartmouth. She went on to Johns Hopkins University, in Baltimore, Maryland, to work on a master's degree. Her work there included writing Native American–themed poetry and short stories. While at Hopkins she stayed in touch with Dorris, and they established a literary relationship, sharing their poetry and writing in letters. After finishing her master's degree in 1979, Erdrich returned to Dartmouth as a writer in residence.

A COLLABORATIVE RELATIONSHIP

In 1980 Erdrich and Dorris began to collaborate in writing short stories. They decided to expand one short story, "The World's Greatest Fisherman," into a novel, which became *Love Medicine*. Their writing relationship also developed into a romantic one, and the two married in October 1981.

Love Medicine tells the stories of the Kashpaws and the Lamartines, two Chippewa families living on a fictional Anishinaabe reservation in North Dakota. The story portrays contemporary Native American life while dealing with issues of identity and the meaning of life. The book makes use of multiple narrators, who shape the story through their different points of view.

Published in 1984 under Erdrich's name, *Love Medicine* was a financial and critical success. Among the many honors it received were the National Book Critics Circle Award for best work of fiction and the American Book Award.

Three more best-sellers followed: *The Beet Queen*, *Tracks*, and *The Bingo Palace*. These novels featured some of the same characters from Erdrich's first novel. But the books also introduced new characters—some from a German-American community living near the fictional reservation.

Erdrich and her husband soon became a well-known literary couple. They typically would work through ideas together and edit each other's work. They collaborated as coauthors in a travel memoir, *Route Two* (1990) and the novel *The Crown of Columbus* (1991).

FAMILY TRAGEDIES

During the 1980s and early 1990s Erdrich and Dorris were raising six children. Three had been adopted by Dorris when he was single—Reynold Abel, Jeffrey Sava, and Madeline Hannah. All of them had been affected by fetal alcohol syndrome—a disability in a child that occurs when the mother abuses alcohol during pregnancy. Erdrich and Dorris also had three daughters together—Persia Andromeda, Pallas Antigone, and Aza Marion.

In the mid-1990s Erdrich and Dorris separated, and she began divorce proceedings. There were allegations of abuse by his daughters and a legal battle was pending.

◀ CROSS-CURRENTS ▶

When Louise Erdrich married Michael Dorris in 1981, he was already the father of three adopted Native American children. To learn more about this award-winning author, turn to page 53.

Many of the novels of Erdrich, who is part Native American and part German, explore cultural identity. She once said, "My fondest hope is that people will be reading me in 10 or 20 years from now as someone who has written about the American experience in all of its diversity."

Severely depressed by the death of his oldest child, which occurred in 1991, and by the accusations against him, Michael Doris committed suicide in January 1997.

STORYTELLER AND BOOK-SELLER

Erdrich has continued to write and publish best-selling and award-winning books. They include *Tales of Burning Love* (1996), *The Antelope Wife* (1998), *The Last Report on the Miracles at Little No* (2001, a National Book Award finalist), and *Four Souls* (2004). Other books include *The Master Butchers Singing Club* (2003), which features German immigrants as its main characters, and *The Plague of Doves* (2008), which is based on the true story of the lynching of three Native Americans.

In addition to writing and raising her children (she gave birth to another daughter, whom she named Azure, in January 2001), Erdrich also runs Birchbark Books. This independent bookstore, founded in 2000, was named after her 1999 children's book, *The Birchbark House*. The store is located in Minneapolis, Minnesota, where Erdrich makes her home.

CHAPTER FIVE

Sherman Alexie: Writer and Filmmaker

S herman Alexie, Jr., is an acclaimed poet and novelist, a screenwriter, a recording artist, and a film director of Spokane and Coeur d'Alene Indian descent. His accomplishments are especially remarkable since he was born with a severe disability—hydrocephalus, or water on the brain. This abnormal accumulation of fluid within the brain causes enlargement of the skull and can result in mental and physical disabilities.

EARLY LIFE

Sherman Alexie was born on October 7, 1966, in Spokane, Washington. At the age of six months, he survived delicate brain surgery.

Sherman Alexie published his first novel, Reservation Blues, *in 1995. He also collaborated with Jim Boyd, a Colville Indian, to record an album of the same name that contains songs from the book.*

THE SPOKANE AND COEUR D'ALENE

Before contact with Europeans the Spokane people lived in the northeastern part of today's Washington State near the Spokane River. White settlers pushed the tribe eastward in the 1880s onto the Spokane Indian Reservation. The tribal headquarters are in Wellpinit, about 50 miles northwest of Spokane, Washington.

Early Coeur d'Alene people lived in villages along the Coeur d'Alene, St. Joe, Clark Fork, and Spokane Rivers in today's northern Idaho, eastern Washington, and western Montana. Their name *Coeur d'Alêne,* or "heart of an awl," came from French fur traders, in recognition of the Indians' sharp trading skills. (An awl is a sharp, pointed tool used to punch holes in leather.)

Instead of being brain-damaged, as doctors had predicted, he was precocious, able to read books at a young age. However, as a child, he sometimes suffered from seizures because of the condition.

Sherman grew up on the Spokane Indian Reservation, in Wellpinit. He has said of himself: "I was a controversial figure on my reservation when I was a kid. I was mouthy and opinionated and arrogant. Nothing has changed."

Kids living on the reservation usually attended Wellpinit High School. Seeking a better education, Alexie chose to commute from his home to high school in Reardan, Washington, about 20 miles south of Wellpinit.

The only Native American at the predominantly white school, Alexie was a key player on the Reardan Indians basketball team. His knack for playing hoops and his good grades earned him a scholarship from Gonzaga University, in Spokane, where he enrolled in 1985. He was the first person in his family to go beyond high school, so his parents and his brothers and sisters pitched in to help with expenses.

Initially planning to become a doctor, Alexie studied for two years at Gonzaga before transferring to Washington State

University, in Pullman. He also switched majors. One of his professors, Alex Kuo, noticed Alexie's talent and encouraged him to write and publish verse. Alexie soon earned critical praise and received fellowships that funded his poetry writing. He also branched out into short fiction.

SUCCESS AS A WRITER

As Alexie's reputation grew, he recognized that a drinking problem that he had developed in college could affect his ability to write. At age 23 he overcame his alcohol addiction and since then has remained sober.

In 1991 Alexie published his first volume, *The Business of Fancydancing: Stories and Poems*. He followed that up with two poetry collections—*I Would Steal Horses* (1992) and *First Indian on the Moon* (1993).

Alexie also published his first collection of short stories in 1993—*The Lone Ranger and Tonto Fistfight in Heaven*. The stories are set on the Spokane Reservation and the main characters are Couer d'Alene boys—Thomas Builds-the-Fire, Victor Joseph, and Junior Polatkin. These same characters would appear as grown men in Alexie's first novel, *Reservation Blues*, published in 1995. In the novel, they put together a rock band called Coyote Springs and try to make a name for themselves off the reservation. Both books were praised for their dark wit and ability to show what it means to be Native American in modern times.

Alexie often uses sharp, biting observations and humor to draw attention to the difficulties American Indians and other minorities still face. He has his share of critics—some of them members of the Spokane tribe on his home reservation who have accused him of mocking them in his stories.

The controversial author scorns writing that is identified as American Indian literature just because its subjects are nature and environmentalism. "You throw in a couple of birds and four

A comedian as well as a writer, Alexie also delivers his stories about contemporary American Indians as standup comedy routines.

directions and corn pollen and it's Native American literature, when it has nothing to do with the day-to-day lives of Indians," he said in an interview. "I want my literature to concern the daily lives of Indians."

SCREENWRITER

In 1998 Alexie tried bringing some modern, everyday American Indians to life onscreen—and scored a hit. His screenplay for the movie *Smoke Signals* drew from characters and situations in his short story collection *The Lone Ranger and Tonto Fistfight in Heaven*. The film was the first to be written, directed, and coproduced by Native Americans: Alexie wrote and coproduced the film and Chris Eyre, who is Arapaho and Cheyenne, served as director and coproducer.

Smoke Signals also featured Native Americans in all the lead roles. It is a comedic buddy movie that follows angry, quiet Victor Joseph, played by Canadian Adam Beach (who is of Saulteaux descent) and quirky, talkative Thomas Builds-A-Fire, played by Evan Adams (who is Coast Salish of British Columbia). The two play Coeur d'Alene Indians who travel from their reservation in Idaho to Phoenix, Arizona, to collect the ashes of Victor's estranged father. Alexie's film about these two seemingly mismatched young men captured the 1998 Sundance Film Festival Audience Award and was a critical and commercial hit.

Alexie wrote and directed another film, *The Business of Fancydancing*, which was released in 2002. The movie, based on Sherman Alexie's book of poetry of the same name,

◀ CROSS-CURRENTS ▶

Born in Canada, actor Adam Beach is a Saulteaux Indian who has played many American Indian roles, including one of the leads in *Smoke Signals*. For more information about this talented actor, turn to page 54.

again featured Evan Adams. He starred opposite Gene Tagaban, who is of Cherokee and Tlingit heritage, in a story of choices and friendship between two men who had grown up together on the Spokane Reservation but then gone their separate ways.

A scene from the 1998 film Smoke Signals, *which featured (from left to right) Monique Mojica, Gary Farmer, and Tantoo Cardinal.*

A NEW AUDIENCE

In 2007 Alexie published his first novel in more than a decade. *The Absolutely True Diary of a Part-Time Indian* was also his first book for young adults. The semi-autobiographical story tells of a teenage boy who decides to leave the Spokane Reservation to attend all-white Reardan High School. The book earned Alexie the National Book Award for Young People's Literature, awarded in November 2007. The young adult novel also garnered the 2008 Boston Globe-Horn Book Award for excellence in Children's Literature.

Sherman Alexie: Writer and Filmmaker

CHAPTER SIX

Irene Bedard: Actress

The daughter of an Inupiat Alaska Native mother and a French Canadian and Cree father, Irene Bedard has had many acting roles. She is well known for giving voice to the title character of the Disney animated feature *Pocahontas*. But this talented actress has given powerful performances in live-action film, too. Among them is her portrayal of Mary Crow Dog in the 1994 television movie *Lakota Woman: Siege at Wounded Knee*. That performance earned her a Golden Globe nomination.

ALASKAN ROOTS

Irene Bedard, whose Inupiat name is Goodiarook (meaning "One who dropped by"), was born on July 22, 1967, in Anchorage, Alaska. She spent her first years in the suburbs of Anchorage, where she grew up learning the stories of her mother's people. At the time, Irene's father held a government job in Anchorage negotiating land rights for Native Americans.

When Irene was eight years old, her family left their home in rural Alaska and moved to Washington State. There, her parents bought a motel, which the young girl helped run. After the motel, the family would own an apartment building, and finally a roller skating rink. Irene also helped out with running the family businesses.

After graduating from high school, Bedard headed to college on the East Coast, where she planned to study physics and philosophy, not acting. Although she had enjoyed writing and putting on plays for her family since she was 10 years old, Irene had never considered becoming a performer. However, she soon changed her mind about acting and enrolled at the University of the Arts in Philadelphia, Pennsylvania. After receiving a bachelor of fine arts degree from the university, she set off for New York City.

EARLY WORK

Eager to create her own opportunities in New York, Bedard helped to found the Chuka Lokali American theater ensemble.

Alaska Native Irene Bedard poses next to a poster for Pocahontas, *the Disney film that helped make her famous.*

The group was made up of other Native American performers who would write their own plays and perform them.

Bedard got her first big role as an actress in the TNT movie *Lakota Woman*, which was based on the 1990 autobiography of Mary Crow Dog. Irene played the young Lakota woman who finds a sense of purpose in her life after becoming active with the American Indian Movement (AIM), a Native American civil rights group. The climax of the film takes place with the 1973 takeover of Wounded Knee, South Dakota, in which more than 2,000 Native Americans protested the past and present actions of the federal government against American Indians. Broadcast on October 16, 1994, *Lakota Woman* was Bedard's breakthrough performance.

Less than two weeks later, the Native American actress appeared in the Disney film *Squanto: A Warrior's Tale,* which also starred Adam Beach. During the filming of *Squanto*, she showed her dedication to her work by choosing not to disrupt the shooting schedule with her wedding. She married her husband, guitarist and songwriter Deni Wilson, on the film set.

POCAHONTAS

In 1994 Bedard was cast to voice the title character of the Disney animated feature *Pocahontas*, released in June 1995. The film was controversial in that it was not an accurate historical depiction of the story of the young Powhatan girl of the early 1600s. According to the diary of John Smith, one of the leaders of the English colony of Jamestown, a 10- to 12-year-old Pocahontas saved him from being killed by the Powhatan tribe. That event occurs in the Disney version; however, Pocahontas is much older. And Smith never made any mention of a romance between the two, as takes place in the Disney story.

Even so, Bedard has said in interviews that she admires the character in the Disney film for being strong-willed and independent. She appreciates the depiction of the Native American woman as a positive one and believes that "Disney's animation has an element of magic."

Bedard also served as the model for the artists who created Disney's heroine. The animators captured her own personality, Irene later said: "My brother came all the way from Alaska to the . . . premiere and throughout the screening, he constantly nudged me because he recognized traits of mine."

Bedard poses with husband Deni Wilson. The two have been married since 1994.

Pocahontas has become a classic, now beloved by fans of all ages, who readily identify Bedard with the strong, beautiful animated Powhatan woman. Irene reprised the role in Disney's 1998 direct-to-video sequel *Pocahontas: Journey to a New World.*

◄ CROSS-CURRENTS ►

Russell Means is a Lakota Sioux who lent his voice to the father in the Disney film *Pocahontas.* In addition to working as an actor, Means has been a longtime activist for Native American rights. To learn more about him, turn to page 54.

Irene Bedard: Actress

TELEVISION AND FILM WORK

Through the years Bedard has appeared in television and film playing both historical and contemporary Native American women. In 1996 she appeared in the HBO television program *Grand Avenue,* which featured modern-day American Indian families living on or near Grand Avenue, in Santa Rosa, California. That was followed by a historical role in the TNT film *Crazy Horse.* Bedard played the lover of the Oglala Lakota warrior who fought the U.S. federal government during the 1870s in the Black Hills War.

In 1998 Bedard played a contemporary Indian woman in *Smoke Signals,* which was written by Native American author Sherman Alexie. She appears as Suzy Song in the small, independent film that won wide acclaim and enhanced her celebrity.

That same year saw the release of *Naturally Native,* in which Bedard played one of three American Indian sisters who confront racism while trying to market their line of cosmetics. The Mashantucket Pequot tribe bankrolled the movie, making it the first film to be wholly financed by tribal money.

Although Bedard has appeared in dozens of movies and voiced characters since *Pocahontas,* she is often associated with that animated character. Things came full circle in 2005 when she appeared in the live-action film *The New World.* It retells the 17th-century story of when the people of Pocahontas's tribe, the Powhatan, first encountered English settlers in today's Virginia. Bedard made a brief appearance in the movie—as Pocahontas's mother.

LIFTING YOUNG SPIRITS

When Bedard is not acting, she can most likely be found singing. Bedard and her husband, Deni Wilson, regularly tour and record. Billing themselves as Irene and Deni, the two perform original contemporary music influenced by elements of Native American, Gaelic, and American culture. Their first release was called *Warrior of Love.*

In 2007 the pair launched a very important collaboration. With support from actor Adam Beach and other friends in the Native American arts community, Bedard and Wilson launched the nonprofit Foundation for the Future of the Seventh Generation. It works to promote education in the performing and media arts for Native American and Alaska Native youth.

At American Indian and First Nations cultural events, Bedard makes the time to speak to her many fans. She tries to deliver a positive message—one that motivates her audiences—she told one interviewer: "What I say depends on the situation, but the basic message I deliver is that you are the only you, through all time, right down to your genetic code. We have this gift of life and everyone has something to contribute."

In the 1998 film Smoke Signals, Bedard plays Suzy Song, a woman who helps one of the main characters of the story, Victor, deal with a troubled family relationship.

CHAPTER SEVEN

Notah Begay III: Pro Golfer

From an early age, Notah Ryan Begay III showed an interest in golfing. Although the odds were stacked against the boy becoming a successful professional golfer, he has done just that. He continues to beat the odds today, battling back from injury on the golf course and using his celebrity to promote happier, healthier lives for Native American people.

OBSESSED WITH SPORTS

Notah Ryan Begay III was born on September 14, 1972, to Notah Begay II, who is of Navajo descent, and Laura Ansera, who is of San Felipe and Isleta Pueblo heritage. When he was two and his brother, Clint, was a newborn, Notah's parents divorced. The boy lived primarily with his mother on the Pueblo of San Felipe, northeast of Albuquerque, New Mexico.

After the divorce Notah would visit his father at his home. The house faced a public golf course that "Note" would enter by slipping through a break in the club's fence. Eventually, Notah II arranged for his golf-obsessed son to do odd jobs on the golf course in exchange for coaching and practice time.

Although he loved golf, Notah III played other sports, too. He enjoyed a traditional game called shinny on the Pueblo of San Felipe, and he was a good basketball player. His athletic ability came in handy when he became the first American Indian male to attend the elite Albuquerque Academy. In addition to attaining national ranking as a junior golfer, the teenager was a star player on his school's basketball team.

Begay next set his sights on academically challenging Stanford University, in Palo Alto, California—and its renowned golf program. After spending extra time on his studies, he made it to the university and became a member of the Stanford Cardinals. There, Begay's traditional hoop earrings and unorthodox playing style (Begay can make shots left- or right-handed) made him stand out on the golf course. His exceptional ability drew the most attention of all, though. A three-time All-American at Stanford, Begay captained the team to the 1994 National Collegiate Athletic Association (NCAA) championship. The team that year included another player who would become a famous golfer—Tiger Woods.

Golfer Notah Begay III looks out over the hills surrounding his Albuquerque, New Mexico, home.

TURNING PRO

After graduating with an economics degree in 1995, Begay turned professional. On the Nike Tour in 1998, he became the third pro golfer to ever shoot a 59 during a tournament. He earned a spot on the 1999 Professional Golfers Association (PGA) Tour, where he continued to distinguish himself. Begay won two PGA tournaments in 1999 and another two in 2000. That same year at the prestigious Master's Golf Tournament he made a hole in one.

Begay's PGA Tour triumphs made him the second Native American golfer ever to win a PGA tournament. A Wintu Indian from California named Rod Curl was the first, in 1974.

IN THE ROUGH

As his likeable nature and exciting golf game won him fans, Begay got into trouble that could have destroyed his reputation. On January 19, 2000, he drove into a parked car while leaving an Albuquerque bar. He was arrested for DWI (driving while intoxicated). At his hearing Begay admitted that he'd been arrested for a DWI in Arizona five years earlier. Had he kept quiet about this, the golfer would have gotten away without jail time, which was mandatory for second offenses.

Although Begay knew it would only make things worse for him, he told authorities about his previous arrest. It was a matter of integrity, he explained in an interview: "It's simple to set a good example if you are succeeding and everything is going your way, but it's tougher when you have to make a decision that could jeopardize a lot of things you've worked very hard for."

The judge sentenced the golf pro to a week in prison, with a daytime work release. This meant Begay golfed or worked

◄ CROSS-CURRENTS ►

Another star athlete with Native American roots is Olympic track and field gold medalist Billy Mills. His performance at the 1964 Tokyo Olympics took the world by surprise. Read his story on page 55.

out during the day, and then checked into jail at night. After his release, he owned up to his mistake whenever he spoke to Native American youth on school visits or in interviews with the press.

While his DWI didn't derail Begay's career, a back injury soon did. In late 2000 the golfer tore two discs in his spine, an injury that made even everyday activities very painful. When he was competing in the Master's in May 2001, he found that the simple act of placing the ball on the tee was agonizing. Begay later attributed the torn discs to overtraining.

A June 1994 photograph of Begay representing the Stanford Cardinals during the NCAA Division 1 Men's Golf Championship, held in McKinney, Texas.

ON THE COMEBACK TRAIL

Still limited by his injury in 2005, Begay turned his attention to helping others. With his father, he founded The Notah Begay III Foundation, which organizes golf programs and soccer leagues for kids in American Indian communities. Although Begay was dealing with depression because of his injuries, he says that watching kids participate in his sports program helped lift his spirits. "I saw the motivation and excitement in their eyes when they played soccer," he said, "and I remembered how much I loved golf."

In 2006 Begay was back on the golf course. He played on the Nationwide Tour, a golf series one tier below the PGA. He spent the first part of 2007 working on his game at European PGA events. However, in May he re-injured his back, cutting his comeback short. In 2008 Begay resumed play after again, doing the hard work of rehab in his new hometown of Dallas, Texas.

HELPING THE COMMUNITIES

Begay has used his recovery time to continue his work in the American Indian community. His foundation's work earned kudos in the fall of 2007, when he was named one of the Institute for International Sport's 100 most influential sports educators. As a spokesman for the Boys and Girls Clubs of America, he has also educated tribal youth on diabetes awareness and prevention.

Begay has parlayed his economics degree and his golf career into founding a company that helps Native American communities develop their economies and increase job prospects on reservations. His business, NB3 Consulting, helps tribes build profitable golf courses and vacation destinations on their lands. "Golf really is a means to a greater end," Begay told *Golf Digest* magazine in 2004.

THE PUEBLO PEOPLE AND THE NAVAJO

Several distinct tribes are considered **Pueblo people**—a Native American group that originated in the Southwestern United States. The San Felipe are based in Sandoval County, New Mexico. The Iselata can be found in the Rio Grande Valley, south of Albuquerque, New Mexico.

The Navajo, also referred to as Diné, or "the people," make up the second-largest Native American tribe in the United States. Most Navajo traditionally live in the Southwest.

Begay putts on the 10th hole during the first round of the AT&T National, held in Bethesda, Maryland, in July 2008.

The deeds of Begay continue to back up his words. In August 2008 he hosted the inaugural Notah Begay III Foundation Challenge (NB3 Challenge) in New York, at the Turning Stone Resort. The fundraiser, which was attended by PGA Tour players such as Steward Cink, Vijay Singh, Mike Wier, and Camilo Villegas, earned $180,000 for health care and wellness programs for Native American youth on Indian reservations.

CHAPTER EIGHT

Martha Redbone: Singer and Songwriter

Martha Redbone is an award-winning musician of Shawnee, Choctaw, Blackfeet, and African American descent. Her music has been described as a blend of Native American and African American roots combined with old-school rhythm and blues, rock, and funk. "Roll Nirvana and Led Zeppelin and Aerosmith up with soul music and then you've got my sound," Martha Redbone has said.

EARLY YEARS

Growing up the daughter of a Shawnee and Choctaw mother and an African American, Lumbee, and Blackfeet father made Martha stand out from the crowd. She spent her childhood in Brooklyn, New York, and in her mother's hometown of Benham-Lynch, Kentucky—a rural town in the Appalachian Mountains. After age 11, she moved to New York permanently.

Martha Redbone performs at the BBC Club in London, England, in 2006.

In Benham-Lynch Martha endured some taunts about her mixed heritage. "Redbone" was a hurtful slang word for someone who was part black, part Native American. Her mother urged her to be proud of being a part of two worlds, but other people's comments still stung.

Martha took piano and guitar lessons as a kid, but she was shy and not a natural performer. Her father was a singer, both in church and in local bands, while her mother loved popular and rock music. But Martha had no plans for a music career: she was content listening to artists such as Prince, Madonna, and other favorites, never dreaming that she would one day make a living writing and singing songs of her own.

THE ACCIDENTAL SINGER

Redbone wanted to be a painter. She moved to London after attending the School of Visual Arts, in New York City. In London she was hired to do some freelance graphic design illustrations for an album. The performer was funk legend George Clinton, who was recording with his band Parliament Funkadelic, or P-Funk. The project was P-Funk's 1996 reunion album, *T.A.P.O.A.F.O.M.* (*The Awesome Power of a Fully Operational Mothership*).

George Clinton and P-Funk at the 1994 Lollapalooza. Redbone jumpstarted a singing career when she was tapped to perform backup vocals for the group's reunion album, released in 1996.

THE SHAWNEE AND THE BLACKFEET NATION

The Shawnee people were formerly native to today's southern Ohio, West Virginia, and western Pennsylvania. During 1830s they were pushed west to the area that is now Kansas, then forced further west to Oklahoma during the 1860s.

Beginning around the 1600s the Blackfoot, or Blackfeet Nation, lived in lands around the Upper Missouri and North Saskatchewan Rivers. The three main tribes were the Siksika (Blackfoot), the Piegan, and the Kainah (the Bloods). Today many Blackfeet Indians live in Montana and Alberta, Canada.

When the band was missing a backup vocalist, a nervous Martha stepped in. Despite her fear, she soon realized that she was born to sing. Walter "Junie" Morrison, a member of P-Funk, thought so, too. He encouraged her to develop her talent. She took lessons to boost her confidence and banish her shyness.

A gifted songwriter, Redbone connected with jazz musician and keyboard player Aaron Whitby and the two became writing partners for music publisher Warner Chappell. They paid their bills by writing songs for other people as they put together a band and began performing. In 2000 they also formed their own production company, called Blackfeet Productions, which she has said was named in honor of her father.

NATIVE PRIDE

In an interview, Redbone explained how she turned something that was once an insult into a source of pride:

> I adopted the stage name Redbone from what my grandmother used to call me, which is a slightly derogatory term for someone of mixed race. I hated it at first but I have a voice now and took the name and am making it into something positive.

Redbone shares her music during the First Annual Native American Blues Festival, held August 4, 2007, at the Okalee Village Amphitheater in Hollywood, Florida.

The artist does not reveal her age, beyond telling a reporter in 2003 that she was "a grown woman." She also keeps her given surname to herself.

Redbone is a singer and songwriter who does it her way. By founding her own production company, she has ensured that her growing fan base can count on every song sounding just the way she intended. Many people agree that Martha's warm, soulful voice and her band's combination of rock, funk, hip-hop blues, and Native sounds are just what they want to hear.

For her self-produced album *Home of the Brave* (2001), Redbone won the 2002 Nammy—the Native American Music Award (NAMA)—for debut artist of the year. "This woman is a true original," gushed *Billboard* magazine, calling her "the kind of artist who sets trends, as opposed to following them."

Skintalk (2004), the followup to *Home of the Brave*, was also well received, winning a Independent Music Award (given by the indie music industry) for best rhythm and blues album in 2006. It also took home an Indian Summer Music Award in the pop category in 2005.

◀ CROSS-CURRENTS ▶

The music of artists working in traditional and contemporary Native American genres is recognized with both Grammy Awards and Nammy Awards. To learn more, turn to page 55.

Although Redbone does not have a big-time recording deal, she is a star among soul and Native sound aficionados. She and her band play at mainstream clubs, Native American music festivals, in tribal casinos, and at reservations.

HELPING OTHERS

Redbone strives to make positive contributions to the world, both on and off the stage. She makes time to teach singing at summer camps for Native American youth, and has plans to open some of her own camps where kids can learn to value their culture and traditions.

Through the National HIV/AIDS partnership Redbone has also helped educate Native and African American young people about human immunodeficiency virus (HIV) infection. As an ambassador for the Global Angels Foundation, she raises funds to help children escape hunger, poverty, and slavery around the world. She believes that it is one of her responsibilities as an artist to help heal problems in the Native American community and in the world.

Redbone is proud of her mixed heritage, she has said, and finds satisfaction that her sound appeals to people of all ethnic groups. "The glamour and the glitz is nice," says Redbone, "but I think success happens in little ways every day. When I look out in the audience when I play, I see every color in the rainbow, and that's what makes me happy."

MINORITIES AND DISCRIMINATION

A 2003 Gallup Poll found that 47 percent of Americans thought that some groups of people in the United States continue to face unfair treatment. The groups facing the most discrimination are African Americans, people in poverty, minority groups, and Native Americans.

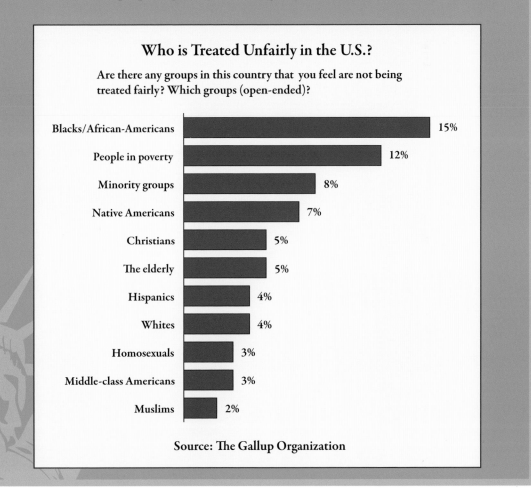

Who is Treated Unfairly in the U.S.?

Are there any groups in this country that you feel are not being treated fairly? Which groups (open-ended)?

Group	Percent
Blacks/African-Americans	15%
People in poverty	12%
Minority groups	8%
Native Americans	7%
Christians	5%
The elderly	5%
Hispanics	4%
Whites	4%
Homosexuals	3%
Middle-class Americans	3%
Muslims	2%

Source: The Gallup Organization

CHARLES CURTIS: FIRST NATIVE AMERICAN VICE PRESIDENT

Charles Curtis was born on January 25, 1860, in North Topeka, Kansas Territory. His mother, Ellen Pappan, was part Kaw Indian and his father, Orren Curtis, was white. When Charles was three, his mother died, and he lived for a time with her Kaw parents on a reservation outside Topeka. But he spent most of his youth with his father's parents in the city.

After graduating from high school in 1876, Curtis studied law and became a lawyer. Passionate about politics, the charismatic Republican won his first public office in 1884 as Shawnee County district attorney. Later elected to the U.S. House of Representatives, he served from 1892 to 1906. During that time he was the main author of the Curtis Act of 1898, an amendment to the Dawes Act that was supposed to protect Indian rights. But it ultimately reduced the power of tribes to govern themselves and control their oil and mineral resources.

Curtis later served in the U.S. Senate, ultimately rising to the position of majority leader. In 1928 he became the first Native American to be elected vice president of the United States when his running mate Herbert Hoover was elected president. After Hoover lost the 1932 election, Curtis retired from politics. He died a few years later, in 1936.

The 31st vice president of the United States, Charles Curtis (1860–1936).

TERMINATION AND RELOCATION PROGRAM

During the 1950s the Mankiller family moved away from Oklahoma as part of the termination and relocation policies of the federal government. The Bureau of Indian Affairs (BIA) encouraged Indians to move off reservations by promising a better life in the cities. In her autobiography, Wilma Mankiller recalls:

> I think Dad initially was opposed to our leaving Oklahoma and our land. As a boy, he had been taken from his home against his will to attend Sequoyah Boarding School. He did not want to leave his community and people again. But he talked it over with some Cherokee friends and eventually he decided it would be a good idea to move. He must have honestly believed that in a distant city he could provide a better life for his children, with all the modern amenities.

The move was hard for Wilma. She noted, "One day I was living in a rural Cherokee community, and a few days later I was living in California and trying to deal with the mysteries of television, neon lights, and elevators. It was total culture shock."

Mankiller noted in her autobiography that the federal program was not a success. Many Native Americans continued to suffer from poverty and poor health after leaving their homelands. Without the support of families and communities, some suffered emotionally and fell victim to substance abuse. Many American Indians who relocated from reservations eventually returned to their communities.

MICHAEL ANTHONY DORRIS

Of Irish, French, and Modoc Indian ancestry, Michael Dorris was a full professor in the Native American Studies Program and the Department of Anthropology at Dartmouth. A celebrated writer, he published 14 books and more than 100 magazine articles and essays.

Dorris was born on January 30, 1945, in Louisville, Kentucky. He graduated in 1967 from Georgetown University, in Washington, D.C., and earned a master's degree of philosophy in anthropology from Yale in 1971. That year, while an unmarried doctoral candidate at Yale University, he adopted the three-year-old Native American boy who would become the subject his most well-known book, *The Broken Cord: A Family's Ongoing Struggle with Fetal Alcohol Syndrome*, published in 1989.

The book recounts how Dorris watched his child grow up developmentally delayed and emotionally disturbed. Eventually the father learned that his child has been affected by fetal alcohol syndrome (FAS)—brain damage caused to a fetus when the mother abuses alcohol. Dorris's book and subsequent testimony before Congress led to the labeling of alcoholic beverages warning of the dangers of drinking during pregnancy. Dorris dedicated *The Broken Cord* to his wife, Louise Erdrich, as the one "who shares this story, who joined me in its living and telling, who made us whole," as well as to Abel Dorris, its subject.

ADAM BEACH

Saulteaux First Nation member Adam Beach rebounded from childhood tragedy to become an acclaimed actor in both his native Canada and the United States. Adam was born on November 11, 1972, in Ashern, Manitoba, Canada. He and his two brothers lived with their parents on the Dog Creek Reserve. When he was eight years old, his mother was killed by a drunk driver. Two months later his father died by drowning. After going to live in Winnipeg, he quit high school to pursue an acting career.

Beach has played both contemporary Indian characters and historical figures. In *Windtalkers* (2002) he played a fictional Navajo serviceman during World War II who is a Code Talker. Although the character was fictional, the story was true: To keep messages from being read by the enemy during the war, the military depended on Code Talkers who used the Navajo language to communicate. In *Flags of Our Fathers* (2006), Beach played a real-life hero of WWII, Pima Indian Ira Hayes (Akimel O'odham) who served as a U.S. Marine paratrooper. That role helped seal his reputation as a serious talent. Beach has also appeared on television—in the 2007 season of *Law and Order: Special Victims Unit* and in the Canadian sitcom *Moose TV*.

RUSSELL MEANS: NATIVE AMERICAN ACTIVIST

Born on November 10, 1939, Russell Charles Means was a young boy when his Oglala Sioux parents, Hank and Theodora, moved to California. They wanted to raise him and his three brothers away from the poverty of South Dakota's Pine Ridge Indian Reservation. The boy would grow up to lend his voice to the struggle for the rights of American Indians.

Means was a key player in the American Indian Movement (AIM), which was founded in 1968 to protest the U.S. government's mistreatment of Native Americans. On February 27, 1973, AIM took over the town of Wounded Knee, the site of one of the most brutal Indian massacres in history. The occupiers demanded reform of the corrupt tribal government of the Pine Ridge Reservation. During the 71-day standoff, Means served as an AIM spokesperson.

Means continues to be involved in activism to protect the rights of Indians. But he has also been active in representing Native Americans in the entertainment industry. His credits include the voice of Chief Powhatan in Disney's animated *Pocahontas* and acting roles in *The Last of the Mohicans* (1992), *Natural Born Killers* (1994), and *Wind Runner* (1995). His many writings include his 1995 autobiography, *Where White Men Fear to Tread*. Means is also a recording artist and performer of protest music.

BILLY MILLS: GOLD MEDAL WINNER

At the 1964 Tokyo Olympics, medal favorite Ben Nighthorse Campbell failed to achieve a gold in judo due to injury. However, in the 10,000-meter race another Native American—an obscure runner named Billy Mills—surprised the crowds by capturing the gold. Mills, an Oglala Lakota orphan from the Pine Ridge Reservation, became the first American to win the Olympic 10K. He had not even been expected to place.

Billy Mills was born June 30, 1938. As a lonely boy at Indian boarding schools, Mills took up running. After helping the track team at the University of Kansas win the outdoor national championships, he failed to qualify for the 1960 Olympic team. He went on to serve in the U.S. Marine Corps, and continued to train for the next Olympics.

In 1964 Mills was a member of the U.S. track and field team competing in Tokyo. When the race of his life began, Mills hung so far back that he did not seem to be in the hunt for a medal at all. He scored his stunning upset by working his way slowly through the pack, and then unleashing a ferociously strong kick in the final stretch of the race.

Mills's story was the subject of the movie *Running Brave,* which was released in 1983. He remains active as an advocate and spokesperson for his people.

GRAMMYS AND NAMMYS

Native American traditional music often incorporates the rhythms and sounds of rattles, whistles, flutes, and drums. Many artists have featured this traditional music in other genres, ranging from rock, to blues, to hip-hop, and to classical music.

In 2001 the National Academy of Recording Arts & Sciences added an award category for Best Native American Music Album to its annual Grammy Awards. Among the artists who have won the Grammy are singer and songwriter Bill Miller, in 2005, for the instrumental album *Cedar Dream Songs* and flutist Mary Youngblood, in 2003, for *Beneath the Raven Moon*, and in 2007, for *Dance with the Wind*.

Since 1998 the Nammys, or Native American Music Awards (NAMA), have recognized the best in all types of Native American music. NAMA Hall of Fame winners include:

1998	Buddy Red Bow (Lakota) and Jimi Hendrix (Cherokee)
1999	Hank Williams (Creek/Cherokee)
2000	Jim Pepper (Kaw/Creek)
2001	Crystal Gayle (Cherokee)
2002	Kitty Wells (Cherokee)
2006	Link Wray (Shawnee)

NOTES

CHAPTER 2

p. 15: "I want to do public policy..." Nadine Brozan, "Chronicle," *New York Times* (November 6, 1992), 5.

p. 16: "It took awhile to..." "Campbell Hails Dedication of Indian Memorial at Bighorn Battlefield," United States Senate Committee on Indian Affairs, June 25, 2003. http://indian.senate.gov/108press/062503.htm

CHAPTER 3

p. 18: "My early childhood in Mankiller Flats..." Wilma Mankiller, "My Home at Mankiller Flats," *Oklahoma Today* (May/June 2004), 42.

p. 19: "When Alcatraz occurred..." Wilma Pearl Mankiller and Michael Wallis, *Mankiller: A Chief and Her People* (New York: Macmillan, 1994), xxiii.

p. 21: "I didn't have a mandate..." Charles T. Jones, "Wilma's Spirit Survives Adversity." *The Cherokee Observer* (August 29, 1999).

p. 22: "community by community..." Wilma Mankiller, "Rebuilding the Cherokee Nation," Gifts of Speech: Women's Speeches from Around the World. http://gos.sbc.edu/m/mankiller.html

CHAPTER 4

p. 24: "where cultures mix and collide." Katie Bacon, "An Emissary of the Between-World," The Atlantic.com, January 17, 2001. http://www.theatlantic.com/doc/200101u/int2001-01-17

p. 25: "Settling into that job..." Michael Schumacher, "Louise Erdrich and Michael Dorris: A Marriage of Minds," *Writer's Digest* (June 1991), 28.

p. 28: "My fondest hope is that..." John Blades, "Louise Erdrich Taps a Slightly Lighter Vein in Quest to Shed Labeling," *Chicago Tribune,* August 31, 1986, 30.

CHAPTER 5

p. 30: "I was a controversial..." Jessica Chapel, "American Literature: Sherman Alexie," The Atlantic Online, June 1, 2000. http://www.theatlantic.com/unbound/interview/ba2000-06-01.html

p. 31: "You throw in a couple of birds..." Quoted in Joelle Fraser, "Sherman Alexie's *Iowa Review* Interview," Modern American Poetry, 2001. http://www.english.uiuc.edu/maps/poets/a_f/alexie/fraser.html

CHAPTER 6

p. 37: "Disney's animation has an..." Renata Joy, "An Interview with Pocahontas," UltimateDisney.com, May 11, 2005. http://www.ultimatedisney.com/pocahontas-interview.html

p. 37: "My brother came all the way from Alaska..." Renata Joy, "An Interview with Pocahontas," UltimateDisney.com.

p. 39: "What I say depends on the situation..." Daniel Gibson, "Little Big Woman: Irene Bedard." *Native Peoples*, November 1, 2000. http://www.

native peoples.com/article/articles/125/1/Actress-Irene-Beddard

CHAPTER 7

p. 42: "It's simple to set a good example . . ." Kelli Anderson, "Notah Begay's Drive," *Stanford Magazine*, May/June 2001. http://www.stanfordalumni.org/news/magazine/2001/mayjun/feature/begay.html

p. 43: "I saw the motivation and . . ." Mandeep Sanghera, "'Soccer' Saved My Career—Begay." BBC Sport/Golf, November 28, 2006. http://news.bbc.co.uk/sport1/low/golf/6190944.stm

p. 44: "Golf really is a means . . ." Guy Yocum, "My Shot: Notah Begay III," *Golf Digest,* October 2004. http://www.golfdigest.com/magazine/myshot_gd0410

CHAPTER 8

p. 46: "Roll Nirvana and Led Zeppelin and Aerosmith . . ." Tracy Dingmann, "Native Pride," *Albuquerque Journal* (November 7, 2003).

p. 48: "I adopted the stage name Redbone from . . ." Sandra Hale Schulman, "Martha Redbone Makes Her Joyful Noise Heard," *News from Indian Country* (October 15, 2002).

p. 49: "a grown woman," Tracy Dingmann, "Native Pride," *Albuquerque Journal.*

p. 49: "This woman is a true original . . ." Larry Flick, "Soul Sistah," *Billboard* (March 9, 2002).

p. 50: "The glamour and the glitz is nice . . ." Tracy Dingmann, "Native Pride," *Albuquerque Journal.*

CROSS-CURRENTS

p. 53: "I think Dad initially was . . ." Wilma Pearl Mankiller, Michael Wallis, *Mankiller: A Chief and Her People*, 69.

p. 53: "One day I was living . . ." Mankiller and Wallis, *Mankiller: A Chief and Her People*, xxii.

GLOSSARY

activism—the practice of taking strong actions, like staging demonstrations, to express one's opinion.

ancestry—one's family or ethnic descent.

assimilation—the blending of one population into another one; the processes of becoming part of a mainstream society or culture.

birchbark—bark of the North American paper birch tree that was used by Native Americans in making canoes, scrolls, containers, and other objects.

boarding school—a school in which students live on the grounds.

Bureau of Indian Affairs—agency of the federal government responsible for administering the Native American lands held in trust by the United States and for providing various health and educational services for Alaska Natives and Native Americans.

conservative—holding to traditional views.

culture—the customs, beliefs, and traditions of a group of people.

discrimination—unjust or prejudicial treatment of a person or group.

epidemic—a rapid, widespread outbreak of disease.

expansionism—a policy of continually enlarging one's territory.

fetal alcohol syndrome—brain damage caused to a fetus when the mother abuses alcohol.

heritage—traits or ways of life passed down from one's ancestors.

indigenous—having originated in a particular place.

liberal—open to new ideas and willing to make changes.

Nammy—Native American Music Award (NAMA).

Olympic Games—international competition staged every four years among the world's greatest athletes who compete as members of national teams.

poll—survey, often conducted over the phone, in person, or over the Internet, in which the public's attitudes about specific issues are documented.

reservation—tract of federal land set aside for American Indians.

severalty—the condition of being separate.

sovereignty—the authority to govern; tribal sovereignty refers to the right of a tribe to govern itself, manage its own property, and regulate its businesses.

tuberculosis—a highly contagious disease that primarily attacks the lungs.

FURTHER READING

Alexie, Sherman. *The Absolutely True Diary of a Part-Time Indian*. Boston: Little, Brown and Company, 2007.

Barrett, Carole, Harvey Markowitz, and R. Kent Rasmussen, eds. *American Indian Biographies*. Hackensack, N.J.: Salem Press, 2005.

Barrows, Sally, ed. *Do All Indians Live in Tipis? Questions and Answers from the National Museum of the American Indian*. Washington, D.C.: Smithsonian Institution, 2007.

Dell, Pamela. *Mankiller: Chief of the Cherokee Nation*. Minneapolis, Minn.: Compass Point Books, 2006.

Edmunds, R. David, ed. *The New Warriors: Native American Leaders Since 1900*. Lincoln: University of Nebraska Press, 2001.

Philip, Neil. *The Great Circle: A History of the First Nations*. New York: Clarion Books, 2006.

Viola, Herman J. *Ben Nighthorse Campbell: An American Warrior*. Boulder, Colo.: Johnson Books, 2002.

INTERNET RESOURCES

http://www.doi.gov/bia/
The government Web site for the Bureau of Indian Affairs, a bureau of the U.S. Department of the Interior, features press releases and useful links.

http://www.fallsapart.com/
The official Web site of Sherman Alexie includes a brief biography, a press section, a calendar of events, and a complete list of publications, recordings, honors, and awards.

http://www.irenebedardanddeni.com/home.html
The official Web site of Irene Bedard and Deni Wilson's band includes articles about Bedard's acting career.

http://www.martharedbone.com/news.html
Martha Redbone's Web site features downloadable songs, a schedule, reviews, and biographical information.

http://www.native-languages.org/kids.htm
Native Languages of the Americas, a nonprofit organization dedicated to preserving Native American languages, hosts this Web site. It includes a master list of American Indian and First Nations tribes and languages, plus an alphabetical list of tribes and their histories.

http://www.nmai.si.edu/
The Web site for the National Museum of the American Indian contains information on its exhibitions, events, and the three museum facilities in Washington, D.C.; New York City; and Suitland, Maryland.

http://www.notah.com/
Notah Begay III's official Web site contains a biography and pressroom, as well as golf stats and information on the Notah Begay III Foundation and his enterprise for tribal land development, NB3 Consulting.

OTHER SUCCESSFUL NATIVE AMERICANS

Fred Begay (1932–): Born on the Ute Mountain Indian Reservation in Colorado, Begay is of Navajo and Ute heritage. He works as a nuclear physicist in alternative energy research.

Joseph Brant (1742–1807): Also known as Thayendanegea, Brant was a Mohawk war chief and commissioned British officer who assisted the British during the American Revolution. After the war, he secured land in Canada for his people.

Tom Cole (1949–): Chickasaw Nation member and Republican member of the U.S. House of Representatives, Cole represents Oklahoma's Fourth Congressional District. He is the only member of Congress who is a registered member of a Native American tribe.

Ada Deer (1935–): Of Menominee (northeastern Wisconsin) descent, Deer is a social worker who became a lobbyist for tribal rights. She is the first American Indian woman appointed to serve as assistant secretary of the Department of the Interior and as head of the Bureau of Indian Affairs (1993–1997).

Vine Deloria, Sr. (1901–1990): A Dakota Sioux, Deloria was an Episcopal archdeacon of South Dakota. He was the first American Indian to reach a top executive position in a major Protestant denomination.

Charles Eastman, or Ohiyesa (1858–1939): A Dakota Sioux, Eastman earned a medical degree from Boston University and became a doctor for the Indian Health Service, in South Dakota.

He was also an author, a political activist, and a cofounder of the Boy Scouts of America.

John B. Herrington (1958–): Born in Wetumka, Oklahoma, Herrington is the first astronaut who is a registered Native American tribal member to fly into outer space (in November 2002, aboard the space shuttle *Endeavour*). The Chickasaw Nation Indian was appointed in 2007 as director of the Center for Space Studies at the University of Colorado at Colorado Springs.

Former assistant secretary for Indian Affairs, Ada Deer became director of the American Indian studies program at the University of Wisconsin—Madison, in 1999.

Phillip Martin (1926–): The chief of the Mississippi Band of Choctaws from 1959 to 2007, Martin helped pull his reservation out of poverty by attracting and developing businesses during his tenure.

D'Arcy McNickle (1904–1977): Born in St. Ignatius, Montana, McNickle was the son of an Irish father and French Cree mother who became a registered member of the Confederated Salish and Kootenai tribes (also known as the Flathead). During his tenure with the Bureau of Indian Affairs he became an expert on U.S. government and Native American tribal relations. McNickle also was an anthropologist, author, and early advocate for Native American rights.

N. Scott Momaday (1934–): An author and English professor of Kiowan heritage, Momaday is the author of *House Made of Dawn,* which won the 1969 Pulitzer Prize for Fiction. He has also served as poet laureate of Oklahoma and in 2007 received the National Medal of Arts, the highest award given to artists by the U.S. government.

Mourning Dove, or Christine Quintasket (circa 1888–1936): Mourning Dove was an Okanogan from the Colville Reservation of eastern Washington who authored the 1927 romance, *Cogewea, the Half-Blood*: *A Depiction of the Great Montana Cattle Range.* It is one of the first novels ever written by a Native American woman.

Leslie Marmon Silko (1948–): An author of Laguna Pueblo, Euro-American and Mexican-American ancestry, Silko gained renown for her 1977 novel *Ceremony*, which features many

A member of the Chickasaw Nation, John Herrington served as a mission specialist for NASA.

traditional stories of the Pueblo people. She is also a poet and writer of nonfiction.

Sitting Bull (circa 1831–1890): As chief and holy man of the Hunkpapa Lakota Sioux, Sitting Bull led the Sioux, Cheyenne, and Arapaho in the 1876 defeat of Lieutenant Colonel George Custer and his troops at the Battle of the Little Bighorn.

Wesley "Wes" Studi (1947–): Born in Tahlequah, Oklahoma, Studi is a Cherokee who has worked in film and television as an actor and director. Among the films he has appeared in are *Dances with Wolves* (1990), *The Last of the Mohicans* (1992), and *The New World* (2005).

Other Successful Native Americans

INDEX

Numbers in **bold italics** refer to captions.

PICTURE CREDITS

ABOUT THE AUTHOR

Kristine Brennan has written numerous books for young people. She lives and works near Philadelphia, Pennsylvania.